I Am Worthy

Empowering Stories & Affirmations to Encourage Healing and Resilience

Compiled by
Dr. Telishia Berry

STRIVE PUBLISHING
www.striveipg.com

Strive International Publishing Group is a division of Courageous Media Group. For more information on the authors, ordering, book signings, or to sponsor an event, contact us at info@courageouswomanmag.com.

Edited/formatted by Shonell Bacon

Publisher/Book Coach – Telishia Berry

Contents

Introduction   1

Affirmations
"I Have Shed My Cocoon"   3
    Tiffany Anthony

"Worthy"   4
    Dr. Shela M. Cameron

"Extra, Extra"   5
    Shawn Cunningham

"The Perfect Moment"   6
    Rev. Allison G. Daniels

"Today…"   7
    Avis Dillard-Bullock

"Strength"   8
    Avis Dillard-Bullock

"I Am…"   9
    Avis Dillard-Bullock

"A Promise"   10
    Jenei Ford

"Positive > Negative"   11
    Jenei Ford

"Release"   12
    Jenei Ford

"Shine!"   13
    Kristee Hall

"Worthy of Breakthrough"   14
   Kimberly Jackson-Jones

"Worthy to Celebrate"   15
   Kimberly Jackson-Jones

"I'm a Praiser"   16
   Kimberly Jackson-Jones

"I Am Resilient"   17
   Sherry Landrum

"I Am Strong Enough"   18
   Sherry Landrum

"Today Is a New Beginning"   19
   Sherry Landrum

"A Chosen Vessel"   20
   Dr. Amicitia Maloon-Gibson

"Worthy of Extraordinary Success"   21
   Dr. Amicitia Maloon-Gibson

"Worthy of Love"   22
   Dr. Amicitia Maloon-Gibson

"I Am Empowered"   23
   Dr. Dianna Maria

"I Am Born to Be Creative"   24
   Marlena Martin

"What's Inside of Me"   25
   Audrey D. Mitchell

"My Value"   26
   Delma Montanez

"Becoming"   27
    Donnetta Moore

"Lifelong Learner"   28
    Donnetta Moore

"Phenomenal"   29
    Donnetta Moore

"Unapologetically Worthy"   30
    Regina Nelson

"I Embrace Resilience with Grace!"   31
    Ashley Nicole

"Trauma-Informed Affirmations   32
for Survivors"
    Dr. Dawn Sheree Paramore

"My Future Does Not Need to Ask   33
My Past for Permission to Exist!"
    Terolyn Phinsee

"Rooted in the Storm"   34
    Dr. Tañia M. Reyes

"Shine On"   35
    Dr. Tañia M. Reyes

"Rainbow"   36
    Dr. Tañia M. Reyes

"What I Can Do through Christ"   37
    Zhelinrentice Scott

"The S.T.A.B.L.E. Affirmation"   38
    Zhelinrentice Scott

"Overcoming Fear"   39
    Shermeaka Settles

"Resilience"   40
    Natalie A. Solomon-Brimage

"Sacred"   41
    Natalie A. Solomon-Brimage

"Evolution"   42
    Natalie A. Solomon-Brimage

"The Disruptor"   43
    Verlisa Wearing

"Divine Love and Purpose Are Keeping Me" 44
    Albertha White Taylor

"Embracing Worthiness"   45
    Katrenia Wright

"Daily Affirmation of Worthiness"   46
    Katrenia Wright

"Being Queen"   47
    Katrenia Wright

Essays
    "Re-claiming My Self-Worth and Successes" 48
        Tiffany Anthony

    "I Am Worthy of Inner Peace"   52
        Dr. Shela M. Cameron

    "A Healing Journey"   55
        Felicia Cox

"Who's That Girl?"   59
    Shawn Cunningham

"There Is No Waste in Waiting"   63
    Rev. Allison G. Daniels

"Is It the Underlying Cause or a Symptom?"   66
    Jenei Ford

"Surviving One of the Darkest Parts   70
of My Life"
    Sherry Landrum

"I Got Up"   73
    Audrey D. Mitchell

"I Am More than Enough"   77
    Donnetta Moore

"Reclaiming Your Worth and Greatness"   81
    Sharrarne Morton

"I Have RA, but RA Does NOT Have Me"   83
    Ashley Nicole

"The Strength of Letting Go"   87
    Dr. Dawn Sheree Paramore

"Bayron Watts, You Are Not Taking   91
My Lunch! Not Today! Never Again!"
    Terolyn Phinsee

"Beyond Betrayal, Hurt, and Pain"   95
    Zhelinrentice Scott

"What Is on the Other Side of Fear?"   98
    Shermeaka Settles

"I Am Enough"   100
    Sharee Williams

"Trust God Always"   102
    Katrenia Wright

Contributors   105

Introduction

In the grand tapestry of existence, every thread represents a unique story woven with strands of resilience, healing, and self-discovery. As the Editor-in-Chief of *Courageous Woman Magazine*, I welcome you to *I Am Worthy: Empowering Affirmations and Stories to Encourage Healing and Resilience*. Within these pages lie narratives of triumph, affirmations of strength, and a guiding light for those navigating the labyrinth of self-worth.

At the heart of this book lies a profound truth: the declaration "I am." It holds transformative power, and adding the affirmations "I have" and "I will" helps to empower each narrative in a world where self-doubt can dim the brightest spirits. This simple act of affirming one's worthiness becomes an anthem of empowerment.

Why are these words so pivotal? Why do they hold the key to unlocking a life of resilience and healing? The answers, as we shall discover, are as multifaceted as the human experience itself.

"I am" affirmations are more than mere words; they are the seeds of positive self-talk, sown in the fertile soil of the mind. With each affirmation, we cultivate a garden of empowerment, nurturing beliefs that blossom into actions and shape our reality.

"I have" affirmations speak to the abundance that resides within each of us. They remind us of the resources, talents, and strengths that we possess, empowering us to face life's challenges with confidence and grace.

"I will" affirmations, meanwhile, cast a hopeful gaze toward the future. They are the promises we make to ourselves, declarations of intention that propel us forward on the journey of self-discovery and growth.

Through the lens of personal narratives and affirmations, *I Am Worthy* invites you on a journey of self-discovery, healing, and growth. Here, you will find stories of triumph over adversity, tales of resilience forged in the fires of life's challenges, and moments of profound transformation.

As we embark on this journey together, let us remember that we are not alone. Within these pages, you will find encouragement from 30 contributors whose goal is to empower you with every word, solidifying the unwavering belief that you are enough just as you are.

So, dear reader, I invite you to join me and these amazing authors on a journey of self-discovery, where the power of "I am," "I have," and "I will" illuminates the path to healing and resilience. For within the pages of *I Am Worthy*, you will find not only daily affirmations and stories, but also the courage to pen your own narrative of empowerment and embrace the truth of your own worthiness.

Telishia Berry

I Have Shed My Cocoon

I will be someone greater than I am now.

The process requires that I shed my old skin and become this new being, getting back to my main principles, rebuilding myself as someone entirely new.

I will soar high just like a butterfly.

But first I will rest in this cocoon, shifting and developing, a complete metamorphosis.

Tiffany Anthony

Worthy

I am worthy of love from within and from those around me.

I am worthy of inner peace, no matter the external circumstances.

I am worthy of respect from myself and others.

I am worthy of self-care and taking time for myself.

I am worthy of achieving my best self and living my best life.

Dr. Shela M. Cameron

Extra, Extra

I am EXTRA, indeed I am. I am Extraordinary.

I am Extra Focused, Extra Empowered, Extra Resilient, Extra Deserving of love, success, and everything I desire.

I am Extra Determined to live the life I want…on my own terms.

I am Extra blessed and favored by God.

I am Extra ready to see all my dreams come to fruition.

Shawn Cunningham

The Perfect Moment

I am in the right place at the right time for God to lead me because the right place, the perfect moment for me is now.

Rev. Allison G. Daniels

Today...

I am worthy of peace.
I am worthy of joy.
I am worthy of love.
>Today I walk in peace knowing that the LOVE of God covers me. The power of God's LOVE strengthens me to walk confidently in peace, joy, and love.

I AM WORTHY...TODAY.

Avis Dillard-Bullock

Strength

I am strong and yet gentle.

I command the room but don't overpower it. I have what it takes, and I take what I have to walk in strength.

I will show up for me and command my space. I walk in strength and live with grace.

Avis Dillard-Bullock

I Am...

I am fearfully and wonderfully made.

I have greatness in me. I walk with strength, courage, and decisiveness.

I will meet this day with the wind at my back, the sun in my face, and the grace of my ancestors that built this place...

I AM.

Avis Dillard-Bullock

A Promise

I am worthy of fully experiencing and expressing my feelings without judgment or suppression and choosing to stand courageously in my vulnerability.

I promise to be kind and compassionate to myself while focusing on the things I am grateful for and appreciate the positive aspects of life no matter how small.

Jenei Ford

Positive > Negative

I am worthy of challenging negative thoughts as they come, replacing them with more positive thoughts, and consciously choosing to shape my mindset toward a more positive perspective that fosters personal growth, healing, and empowerment.

Jenei Ford

Release

I am able to release past traumas, negative beliefs, and let go of anything that hinders my personal growth to create space for new beginnings and purposeful experiences.

I promise to embrace and accept my imperfections as part of my journey and explore authentic experiences that define me as a uniquely designed individual.

Jenei Ford

Shine!

I shine because I AM...
...beautiful!
...wonderful!
...powerful!
...divine!

I am a role model for girls, ladies, and those standing on the front lines! I set high standards, boundaries, and expectations. I am living up to my maximum potential!

I am boundless!

I am limitless!

I am forever fearfully and wonderfully made!

Kristee Hall

Worthy of Breakthrough

I AM worthy of BREAKTHROUGH.
   I HAVE discovered that I have a right to be free.
   NO MORE bondage.
   The yoke has been destroyed off my neck and my family, friends, and loved ones.
   The price has been paid.
   So, I WILL walk in my newfound deliverance.

#LetzMakeJESUSFamous

Kimberly Jackson-Jones

Worthy to Celebrate

I AM worthy to celebrate - Declare out loud: "I Did That!"

I HAVE completed those tasks, accomplished those goals, and walked through those impossible doors.

Now, I WILL do even greater because of what HE said about me: that I'm EMPOWERED, the Apple of HIS eye, and will do even greater works!

#LetzMakeJESUSFamous

Kimberly Jackson-Jones

I'm a Praiser

I AM worthy to be a PRAISER - Why? "Because that's what I do!"

I PRAY no matter what it looks like, PRAISE while in turmoil, and WORSHIP though I feel defeated.

I HAVE FAITH that miracles, the impossible made possible, take place because of PRAISE.

That's why I WILL always have a PRAISE on my lips and a clap in my hands.

#LetzMakeJESUSFamous

Kimberly Jackson-Jones

I Am Resilient

I am embracing setbacks, not as roadblocks but as opportunities.

I am looking adversity in the face and drawing strength from within, navigating life's tumultuous currents.

I am bouncing back from challenges and push forth onto stepping stones of growth because God has equipped me.

Sherry Landrum

I Am Strong Enough

I am strong enough because my potential is limitless, and I will always be evolving.

I am overcoming any challenges that are presented to me, and my confidence is growing as each day passes.

I have overcome every obstacle put before me because it leads to my growth and success.

Sherry Landrum

Today Is a New Beginning

I will start each day fresh as it opens up new possibilities.

I will embrace positive growth, keep nurturing my mindset, and cultivate meaningful relationships, seeing positive changes each day.

I will find joy in the small moments.

I will embrace and live in my God-given purpose, bringing fulfillment to my life and those around me.

Sherry Landrum

A Chosen Vessel

I am a chosen vessel and servant leader in God's Kingdom.

I have the internal fortitude to handle the naysayers and negativity.

I will keep God first, my family second, and close friends and relationships as priorities.

God is my source of spiritual wisdom, knowledge, and understanding to bind anything that's not of God in Earth.

Dr. Amicitia Maloon-Gibson

Worthy of Extraordinary Success

I am worthy of extraordinary success.

I have unlimited gifts of experience, wisdom, and spiritual foundation.

I will walk with unshakable faith, diligently accomplishing everything I dream I have because I am equipped and empowered to do so.

Fear cannot stop me from moving forward because I can do all things through Christ who strengthens me daily in my faith walk.

Dr. Amicitia Maloon-Gibson

Worthy of Love

I am worthy of love.

I have the power to love others unconditionally and those I love know and understand this Fruit of the Spirit that resides within me.

I will walk in spiritual gifts every day, expecting nothing in return.

God loves me unconditionally, even at times when I am not worthy enough to receive His unconditional love.

Dr. Amicitia Maloon-Gibson

I Am Empowered

I AM EMPOWERED!

I have a stellar character that continues to foster positive relationships personally and professionally.

I am a thought-provoking leader who brings out remarkable skills in other people.

I am unapologetically in a state of congruence where my actions, decisions, and intentions are all connected to my overarching goals and values.

I will continue to be grateful for my continued knowledge and insight, which helps me navigate through difficult situations.

Dr. Dianna Maria

I Am Born to Be Creative

I am woman. God gave me the power to house and create a whole new life. Ever resilient, through pain even, I can create, birth, and produce.

I am born to create! There is no woman who cannot rise from the ashes to recreate herself. I am the joyful keyholder of the INCREDIBLE ability to recreate myself and my life!

Marlena Martin

What's Inside of Me

I am worthy enough to live the quality of life that God promised me.

I have everything inside of me to achieve happiness, abundance, peace, and freedom until it overflows in every area of my life.

I WILL have what I say because I am ENOUGH!

Audrey D. Mitchell

My Value

I am worthy of respect and honor. My value is far above all the riches in this world.

I am a blessing, a gift, and a treasure on this earth. Time works in my favor. Excellence is always achievable because I master the basics: confidence, respect, wisdom, and assertiveness. I am kind, compassionate, and empathetic toward me.

Delma Montanez

Becoming

I am excited about the woman that I'm becoming because I fought to become her. SHE IS ME!

Donnetta Moore

Lifelong Learner

I will continue to learn from experiences and strive to become the best version of myself.

Donnetta Moore

Phenomenal

I am Powerful, I am Resilient, I am Successful, I am Strong, I am Educated, I am Fearless…I am a Phenomenal Woman.

Donnetta Moore

Unapologetically Worthy

I am worthy! I was *born* worthy!

My worthiness is not determined by the things in life I had to endure. My worthiness is determined by every obstacle I have overcome in my life. It's my inner core that is unshakeable and unstoppable.

I will never forget that I am worthy of it all, and I'm going after everything that belongs to me.

End of story!

Regina Nelson

I Embrace Resilience with Grace!

I am complete and abundant, equipped with everything I need to succeed, regardless of the challenges my chronic illness presents.

I harness my strength, courage, and resilience to RISE above any circumstance, transforming my pain into a purposeful and powerful force.

I honor my body as a sacred temple, acknowledging its strength and capability.

Ashley Nicole

Trauma-Informed Affirmations for Survivors

I am resilient and strong!

I emerge from trauma with exceptional wisdom and courage.

I empower myself daily to heal, grow, forgive, and transform my experiences into strength and inspiration.

My trauma does not define me.

I am a survivor, unapologetically overcoming all odds.

Each step I take is a testament to my resilience and healing abilities.

I AM enough.

Dr. Dawn Sheree Paramore

My Future Does Not Need to Ask My Past for Permission to Exist!

I am present.

I will no longer dwell on my past mistakes and failures. I choose today to move forward. If I look back, I take away from rebuilding a better me.

I will start where I am right now! Attention, past, my future doesn't need your permission to exist.

Terolyn Phinsee

Rooted in the Storm

I am strong like rooted trees surviving a storm. Strong-rooted trees survive storms and bloom in the spring.

Be strong and firmly rooted so when the storm passes not only do you get trimmed of the dead weight, but you also have the chance to bloom greater.

Dr. Tañia M. Reyes

Shine On

I am shining like the brightness of the sun as it rises every day.

I am choosing to rise and shine brightly as I conquer everything that comes my way. I don't have to see the brightness of the sun to know it is shining behind the clouds.

Dr. Tañia M. Reyes

Rainbow

I will be a reflection of all the brightness in my life like a rainbow.

A double rainbow is caused by light being reflected on a mere drop of water twice before leaving it. No matter how small the positive is in my life, I will use it to reflect double the greatness.

Dr. Tañia M. Reyes

What I Can Do through Christ

I AM living in integrity: I can do all things through Christ Who strengthens me.

I AM lacking no good thing because I seek ye first the kingdom of God and his righteousness, and all these other things will be added until you.

I WILL walk by faith and not by sight, ever hopeful and pursuing the realization of my dreams.

Philippians 4:13, Matthew 6:33, 2 Corinthians 5:7

Zhelinrentice Scott

The S.T.A.B.L.E. Affirmation

I am a **s**piritual being, fully **t**hankful for all of my **a**bundant **b**lessings, and brave to walk in **l**ove no matter what adversity comes my way. I am **e**quipped to follow and achieve my dreams.

Zhelinrentice Scott

Overcoming Fear

I will not let fear and anxiety hinder me from fulfilling my divine purpose.

Shermeaka Settles

Resilience

I AM an unyielding lighthouse, courageously navigating through life's transformative storms, each one sculpting the contours of my path.

I champion the essence of self-care, placing my well-being at the forefront as I traverse through adversity.

Every challenge serves as a steppingstone to profound self-awareness and fortified resilience.

I am SHE: the epitome of unwavering strength and relentless determination.

Natalie A. Solomon-Brimage, MPH

Sacred

I AM the master architect of my sacred sanctuary, a harmonious fusion where vulnerability meets creativity and spirituality soars.

In my quest to forge a deep, soulful connection, I embody the very essence of this sacred space.

It mirrors my inner tranquility and the path I tread, encapsulating the boundless imagination and deepest desires of my soul.

I AM HER.

Natalie A. Solomon-Brimage, MPH

Evolution

I AM the embodiment of exploration and enlightenment, meticulously crafting sanctuaries for my own evolution.

I serve as a beacon of hope and wisdom, illuminating paths for others by generously sharing the saga of my healing.

My journey, adorned with trials, unwavering faith, and formidable resilience, steers me toward ultimate well-being.

Natalie A. Solomon-Brimage, MPH

The Disruptor

I am a disruptor of mediocrity!
I refuse to settle for ordinary and seek to challenge the status quo!
I strive for excellence in everything that I do.
I will achieve extraordinary results that stand out from the rest.

As I embrace this mindset, I will make a big impact on the world and leave a lasting legacy.

Verlisa Wearing

Divine Love and Purpose Are Keeping Me

I am safe with God. God is love. I am loved, and I am loveable.

Pure love is sweet and kind. It is peace and joy. I deserve this beautiful gift. I was birthed by this beautiful gift, and I am worthy of this beautiful gift.

I have released shame and guilt. I forgive myself. I am strong. I am complete. I am enough. I am worthy.

Albertha White Taylor

Embracing Worthiness

I am worthy. I deserve my heart's desires. I am willing to do the work to make them mine, even in my darkest moments.

Katrenia Wright

Daily Affirmation of Worthiness

I will ask God for happiness, acknowledging his greatness. Each day, I'll affirm, "I am worthy, capable of growth and destined for success."

Katrenia Wright

Being Queen

I will treat myself kindly, with honesty and consideration, understanding that happiness comes from within. I affirm that I am a queen, capable of shining and committed to evolving.

Katrenia Wright

Re-claiming My Self-Worth and Successes
Tiffany Anthony

I am flying high in my richness after trusting and believing in my self-worth and successes. Do you really understand your sense of self-worth? Understanding your self-worth is very important in identifying who you really are. Once you identify your self-worth, you can then continually grow as a person. How we measure our worth and how we see ourselves is the crux of something called courage, confidence, learning from failures, and our success. For me, my self-confidence and the ability to act courageously always depended on my self-esteem (or self-worth), my thoughts on myself, and my character.

<u>Self Confidence</u>

Self-confidence to me is the act of taking an initiative whereas self-esteem is more general and focuses on how you see yourself personally and how we value those thoughts. These thoughts can vary from person to person. One person's self-esteem can be weighed by getting approval from others. On the other hand, some may base it on relationships (friends, family, work, spouse, etc.). I had very low self-esteem because of the people around me. They themselves were not confident; therefore, they didn't know how to teach me and ultimately tore me down with negativity. As I started to work on developing myself, it was important for me to check in on my self-esteem because my level of self-esteem determined how confident I was in the actions I took. The two go hand and hand.

Knowing Your Worth

Because of my experiences, I've learned over the years what it means to identify if you have a healthy or low self-esteem. If your worth is healthy (i.e., loving yourself beyond your successes and knowing your worth), your confidence will grow. It took me a long time to accomplish this, but in the end, I persevered. There are failures, such as relationships or a job not working out, but knowing your value allows us to have confidence that these failures are not a reflection of who we are as a person. On the other hand, if you transmit low self-esteem, most likely you will think negative thoughts like I once did (i.e., asking myself what's wrong with me or why I couldn't do anything right).

Doubt

Negative thoughts encourage doubt to rear its ugly head, and when we doubt ourselves, it's difficult to handle certain situations. If something doesn't go the way you wanted, you might question yourself as a person: *Did things go wrong because something is wrong with me?* Now, don't confuse healthy self-esteem with high self-esteem because you'll start thinking you're this phenomenal person when you're actually channeling low self-esteem. This can be counterproductive or arrogant, so make sure you're taking care of your emotional needs. I focused on remedies that work for me, such as making lists of goals and crossing them off when they were achieved. Try thinking of remedies that work for you. If you focus on perfecting that skill, the fear of failure won't penetrate as much.

Fill That Void

In addition to caring for your emotional needs, checking in on your physical needs is just as vital. These days, my health has become very important in my life. Having experienced a chronic illness to the point where nothing gave me joy, I found a new perspective on what's really important to me, and that's feeling mentally and physically healthy. As I didn't understand the importance of my health, I would frequently put my career and family first. I thought it was emotionally satisfying, but this gave me a false sense of achievement and satisfaction. Although we don't always like to admit, we often resort to family and work to fill that void. I know I certainly did.

Ending Cycles

I would sometimes fall into the trap of thinking my appearance and net worth measured how good of a person I was. However, doing so is like aiming at a moving target; you'll never hit it. If your self-worth is linked to your net worth or appearance, and you compare yourself to others, you can start to feel your more valuable than your peers. We sometimes measure our success and emotions by others' successes and treasures. We quickly learn how that perception can change continually. Let's stop this endless cycle.

People Pleaser

By the same token, we all have that person(s) to whom we say, "Your opinion means the world to me." Instead of doing that, stand in front of the mirror and say it to yourself. I had to realize I am that person, and my opinion mattered the most. Finally, STOP BEING A PEOPLE PLEASER (I once was). It's time to be courageous and take control of our values and successes. These are some of the behaviors we manifest when we become a people pleaser.

- You find it hard to say no.
- You find yourself agreeing with people, or at least pretending to agree to avoid confrontation.
- You apologize even if you haven't done anything wrong.
- You consider everyone else's feelings before your own.
- You put most people's needs before yours.
- You don't speak up if you're hurt in a situation because you don't want anyone to feel bad.

Self-Pleaser

Instead of being a people pleaser, be a SELF-PLEASER. These are some of the behaviors we have to manifest when measuring our self-worth. (Write down what each of these mean to you.)

- I will put God first.
- I will treat others with respect.
- I will have empathy.
- I have integrity.
- I have self-respect and honor my feelings.
- I am supportive and reliable.
- I am honest and true to myself.
- I will handle tough times gracefully.

Given these measures, our self-worth and our successes will become more transparent. By doing this work, it will enhance our self-esteem, self-worth, and successes. In the end, a warrior will always find strength to exude one's self-confidence and enhance the chances of life's successes. This is where I started and now, I have incorporated this in my daily practice. This has made my life overall happier, healthier, more honorable, and because I am being true to myself, I have nurtured better relationships, more integrity, and more respect for others.

I Am Worthy of Inner Peace
Dr. Shela M. Cameron

As a newly turned 60-year-young woman, I am worthy of the many achievements, accolades, awards, and retirement I have received. My mother's solid advice was very inspirational and instrumental in guiding me through my life and career. As a child, I was always a giver and leader. Once I graduated from high school, became an adult, graduated from college, joined the military, became a parent, opened two businesses, received my PhD, became an author, and earned over a million dollars, I knew I was wealthy spiritually, mentally, physically, and financially. My mother, the wind beneath my wings, always told me to pray, keep my head, hang in there, and that everything was going to be alright. I will never forget the two scripture that she gave me from the Bible:

- Matthew 7:12, Do unto others as you would have them do unto you.
- Luke 12:48, To whom much is given much is required.

In addition to the strong and worthy advice from my mother, I discovered a saying that deeply resonated with me: *Tough times don't last forever but tough people do.* My story, which is one of self-discovery, healing, challenges and transition, personal development, and knowing that I am enough and can handle life changes, epitomizes this saying.

When I was 25 years old, I joined the Army National Guard to pay off the balance of my college loan. My obligation was to serve six years for one weekend a month and two weeks out of the year. I was happy to accept the offer so that I could take the financial burden off my parents; therefore, I signed the dotted line. This was the beginning of my military career and my first time flying.

It was at this time that the first scripture hit me, Luke 12:48.

I went and graduated from basic and advance individual training in Fort Jackson, South Carolina, a Private First Class (PFC). Upon returning, I worked diligently to be promoted to the next rank of E-4 Specialist. I soon accomplished that rank and desired for more challenges and responsibility to be able to lead, make changes, mentor, and help others. At this point, I applied and tested to become an officer. To my surprise, I failed with a score of 89, when the passing score was 90. I had to wait six months to retest. When that time came around, I took the test a second time, and once again, I failed with the same 89 score. I was really surprised, even more so because I have a photographic memory and realized that the test was the same except for the questions being in a different order. I was very puzzled yet determined more than ever to take and pass the test within the next six months.

Another six months passed, and I failed a third time and was told by the examiner that sometimes some people can't be leaders nor are cut out to be an officer. I was furious at his belittlement. As I stormed out the door, I yelled, "You can bet your last dollar I'll be back and pass."

Nearly two years had passed with me trying to get into the officers academy, but on the fourth try, lo and behold, the examiner came out of the office and said, "Congratulations, you finally passed with a ninety."

I was relieved and knew at that moment I had emerged out of resilience to keep coming back to take the test. I began the class and attended it with 36 other candidates. There were 19 Caucasians and 17 African Americans. Of the African Americans, nine were males and eight were females. When our 16 weeks of officer training was over, the class only graduated 15. The graduates comprised 13 Caucasian males, one Caucasian female, and *only one* African American and female, ME!

As we all graduated and went our separate ways to take on different assignments, I always kept in my mind that I Am Enough. We lost contact, but over the years, we reconnected. Throughout my career, I made it my best intention to ensure that I supported, assisted, and helped others in any way I could. Over time, the second scripture, Matthew 7:12, hit me. I am proud to say that after serving 34 years active duty in the United States Army as a lieutenant colonel, I am the last one standing among my fifteen graduate peers. I proudly take my seat at the table on March 31, 2024, Easter Sunday as I Rise in Retirement, for I AM WORTHY, and through my proven worthiness, I have achieved personal success and helped others with courage, conviction, and integrity.

A Healing Journey
Felicia Cox

My healing journey is a testament to unwavering resilience and triumph over profound adversity. I am a wife, mother, professional bodybuilder, and entrepreneur. My odyssey began in August 2016 when I decided to undergo surgery to address fibroid tumors that had plagued me since the age of 18. Despite medical advice to leave them be, the pain had become unbearable. Choosing the path of ablation of the cervix, I initially found relief, but the respite was short-lived. The pain returned with a vengeance, leading me to consult a gynecologist, who recommended a hysterectomy without exploring other options. This decision set the stage for a complex surgery that took an unexpected turn, lasting six hours due to complications.

Emerging from surgery, I discovered that my bladder had been inadvertently cut, a revelation delivered with surprising nonchalance by my doctor. The subsequent weeks involved living with a catheter, facing uncertainty, and enduring emotional and physical turmoil. As complications persisted, my journey took a toll on my mental health. Battling anxiety and depression, I faced moments of despair. Yet, God's voice guided me through the darkest thoughts. Having a supportive family and faith played crucial roles in my perseverance.

The saga continued with multiple attempts at bladder repair, each accompanied by its set of challenges. Catheters, uncontrollable urination, and a prolonged period of healing became my daily reality.

The physical and emotional toll was immense, leading me to a yearlong recovery.

Amidst the struggle, I found solace in self-help literature, spiritual music, and motivational content. These resources, combined with a strong support system, became my lifelines during moments of anxiety and despair. The journey to recovery wasn't just physical; it became a battle for mental strength and emotional well-being.

After months of setbacks, my persistence paid off. The surgery to repair my bladder was successful, marking the beginning of my physical recovery. However, the emotional scars lingered, manifesting as anxiety and depression. Determined to reclaim my life, I embarked on a path of self-discovery and transformation.

My recovery involved overcoming anxiety and depression and pushing myself to reclaim my strength. Starting with just 10 minutes on the treadmill, I gradually increased my endurance, both mentally and physically. Encouraged by inner strength, I committed to do a bodybuilding competition; a dedicated diet and eight months of training resulted in significant transformation. The journey to the stage was not just about physical fitness but a testament to my inner strength. Against all odds, I competed *and* emerged victorious, winning first place and securing multiple pro cards on a national stage.

My triumph goes beyond the glitz of competitions. It extends to my role as a coach, inspiring others with my story of turning pain into passion. Today, I stand as a beacon of hope, emphasizing the importance of patience, perseverance, and the unwavering belief that healing is not only possible but deserved.

As I continue to coach and uplift others worldwide, my story serves as a reminder that in the face of seemingly insurmountable challenges, the affirmation "I am worthy of healing" can be a guiding force toward resilience, transformation, and triumph.

As you embark on your journey of healing and resilience, I invite you to consider the following empowering principles drawn from my personal story:

- **Informed Decision-Making**
  - o Seek Multiple Opinions: In matters of health, especially when facing medical procedures or treatments, empower yourself by seeking multiple opinions from qualified healthcare professionals. Your health is a collaborative effort, and diverse perspectives can contribute to more informed decisions.
- **Holistic Approach to Health**
  - o Mind-Body Connection: Acknowledge the profound connection between your physical and mental well-being. Explore and adopt holistic strategies that address both aspects of your health. This integrated approach can pave the way for a more comprehensive and enduring recovery.
- **Building a Support System**
  - o Lean on Loved Ones: Surround yourself with a robust support system that includes family, friends, and faith communities. The emotional and practical support from those who care about you can be a source of strength during challenging times. Remember, you don't have to navigate this journey alone.
- **Coping Strategies**
  - o Explore Resources: Discover and implement coping mechanisms that resonate with you. Whether it's delving into self-help literature, finding solace in

uplifting music, or drawing inspiration from motivational content, these tools can provide comfort and guidance during moments of emotional turbulence.

- **Goal Setting for Recovery**
  - o Small Victories Matter: Embrace the power of setting small, achievable goals on your path to recovery. Each milestone, no matter how seemingly insignificant, is a victory that contributes to the larger picture of your healing journey. Celebrate these moments, and let them fuel your determination.

Remember, your healing journey is unique, and it is shaped by your choices and resilience. By integrating these principles into your approach, you can cultivate a mindset of empowerment, self-discovery, and transformative healing. As you navigate the challenges ahead, know that you have the strength within you to overcome, and each step forward is a testament to your courage.

Who's That Girl?

Shawn Cunningham

Inside a fourth-grade classroom, a confident little Black girl with a light in her eyes answered a question asked by her teacher.

"Shawn, what do you want to be when you grow up?" asked Miss Woodruff.

The little girl responded, "When I grow up, I want to be Miss America."

"Well, that probably won't happen, not for you."

"Yes, it can," the little girl said. "My parents said I can be whatever I want when I grow up."

A frown formed on the teacher's face as she yelled at the girl, "Are you calling me a liar? How dare you answer me back. You think you're so smart. You're not! And just for doing that, no one will talk to you, and I won't call on you. You'll sit there and be quiet, be invisible."

And with that, my life changed. I was scared and scarred. Something happens when your name is taken from you. You cease to exist. It's like that scene from *Roots*, when the slave master brutally whips Kunta Kinte into accepting the name Toby. When he finally relents, his identity is stolen. His spirit is broken. I would spend much of my life trying to overcome that painful experience.

And it opened the door to more pain…being bullied and abused in school and relationships. It hurt the biggest relationship anyone can have: the perception of and the relationship you have with yourself. I teetered between portraying that confidence but not too much, lest people end up hating me.

Most kids start out confident, but the realities of life, the negative experiences, and the endless opposition and criticism tear at that self-confidence, their self-esteem. It destroys not only your dreams but also the ability to fuel them.

I watched Vanessa Williams win Miss America, then Debbye Turner, Marjorie Judith Vincent. They were *beautiful, poised, confident,* and *Black*...like me! I thought, *I want to be just like them!* To no avail. I unsuccessfully competed in the Miss America system for years. Truthfully, I wasn't ready to win. I was an imposter syndrome amnesiac the entire time. The judges could see right through that. The only person I fooled was myself. It's tragic when you feel uncomfortable in your own skin.

A beloved pageant coach spoke some hard truths to me when he said, "Shawn, who are you? Why should the judges pick you when you won't even pick you? You're trying to be all these winners. They already won Miss America! How about just being you?"

The same went for my television career. The industry knew Oprah, Barbara Walters, Katie Couric, Savannah Guthrie. But it needed to know Shawn Cunningham.

That was a harsh mirror reflecting at me. One I wasn't ready to see.

While working in Florida, I allowed a now ex-boyfriend to slither into my life. It was an abusive relationship that lasted a year. It was also a relationship that could have had a very different ending. One night, he stabbed me in the leg. I lay bleeding, frightened, pleading for my life. He threatened to dump me in the Everglades and leave for me for dead for gators or snakes to kill me and never be seen or heard from again.

That was my low point. I was 70 pounds, had zero self-worth, was completely ashamed. I was reporting the news, and nobody knew what I was enduring behind closed doors. I prayed for God to get me out of that.

And HE did.

I came back to New York, got myself into therapy, and started to look at what role I played in everything that had happened. The hard truth is was I didn't like myself much or at all. I didn't think I deserved better.

"Say My Name, Say My Name…"

Nothing would change until I was ready for change, and that change began when I met my now husband, lifelong soulmate, and best friend AJ. With him, I was finally seen, accepted, and unconditionally loved. For years, I was stuck. My light was diminished. But it wasn't dead. Inside me was a determination to persevere.

Granted, he had to work hard to break down my walls. But the point is he kept doing so. He showed me I was worth it. Then it dawned on me, *I was.*

The past 20 years have been a journey of self-discovery, self-acceptance, and self-assurance. Taking ownership of my name, my voice, my narrative. Falling in love with myself, knowing I was more than enough.

When I'm quiet and still, I hear God speaking truths unto me. I am divinely made and highly favored. I am not cursed! I am worthy! I deserve all good things. I deserve love, to be loved, and give love. My life has value and meaning. My voice is important. I have a right to be heard. God doesn't make mistakes. He created me with a purpose. My dreams may be delayed, but they are always destined to come true. I have few regrets, nay two...that I didn't have my *A-ha!* moment sooner. If I had, I wouldn't have ever allowed anyone to violate me or nearly kill me. In rewriting the narrative Miss Celie says in *The Color Purple* to better suit me, I declare, *I'm great, I'm worthy. I'm Black, and I am most definitely beautiful. Dear God, thank you...I'm here.*

Ultimately everything is a choice, to be miserable or to be happy. Choose happiness.

I've come into my own. And while the world now knows and says my name, (the side benefit of being a public person), the name I'm most proud of is *Mom*. God gifted us a beautiful son. Learning from my own life experiences, I *champion* his being vocal, curious, outgoing, and confident. There is greatness in him, as there is in me.

I overcame a great deal to become the winning woman I am today. People have new names for me: TV anchor, talk show host, community leader, changemaker, proud wife, proud mom, survivor, success story, *QUEEN!*

And whatever name anyone calls you, the one that matters most is the one you call yourself, the one you answer to.

There Is No Waste in Waiting
Rev. Allison G. Daniels

"I waited patiently for the Lord; and he inclined unto me, and heard my cry."
Psalm 40:1 KJV

Initially, when my husband and I were first married, our plan was to have our first baby together, *after* we purchased our first home. However, after four miscarriages, we believed, unfortunately, that this would never happen to us. Yes, we assembled in prayer many nights together, and we were committed to attending church and seeking God first and foremost, together, in hopes of Him hearing and answering our prayer.

We made sure that we intentionally exercised regularly, and we both welcomed a nutritious diet, hoping, thinking that if there was something more, we could do to make this beautiful life come about, it would surely come to pass. Of course, as we later came to understand, this was totally out of our control. But, nonetheless, while on the expectancy journey, we believed it would happen for us because God had already blessed us with our first daughter although she was not my husband's biological daughter; she was still *our* beloved daughter. Yes, she is both our humble pride and joy, and we wanted to bless her with a sibling.

Since that never happened for us (during that waiting timeframe), I began to think I wasn't worthy enough to conceive again. I began to ponder and believe that God just was not going to bless us because He had already done so much for us. Then, low self-esteem began to creep and settle in, taking up residence, causing me unwanted pain and anxiety, but nevertheless, I knew God was present even in my brokenness and that His timing was not our timing, but nonetheless, I was hurting. So, slowly I had to start speaking life-changing words over my situation and over my body—our bodies.

As you're reading this today, some of you might be concerned or worried or even anxious about a situation or challenge you are currently facing. Maybe you are concerned about your future. Know that God has you covered and that He will answer your prayers in His time and in the right season of your life.

Today, I share with you the scriptures that carried me in my season of patiently waiting, one of which was the Prayer of Jabez:

- <u>1 Chronicles 4:10</u>: *And Jabez called on the God of Israel, saying, Oh that thou wouldest bless me indeed, and enlarge my coast, and that thine hand might be with me, and that thou wouldest keep me from evil, that it may not grieve me! And God granted him that which he requested.*

- <u>Deuteronomy 28:1-4</u>: *And it shall come to pass, if thou shalt hearken diligently unto the voice of the Lord thy God, to observe and to do all his commandments which I command thee this day, that the Lord thy God will set thee on high above all nations of the earth: 2 And all these blessings shall come on thee, and overtake thee, if thou shalt hearken unto the voice of the Lord thy God. 3 Blessed shalt thou be in the city, and blessed shalt thou be in the field. 4 Blessed shall be the fruit of thy body, and the fruit of thy ground, and the fruit of thy cattle, the increase of thy kine, and the flocks of thy sheep.*

So, during my next doctor's visit, just to give it another try, I went in for my annual physical, and they ran additional tests.

Although I was hopeful and really saturated in prayer, I still reserved a bit of doubt, unbelief; you know, just in case it didn't happen just yet.

But God! But God! But God! Glory to God!

Sometime after that journey, God eventually blessed us with our precious daughter when we were not expecting to conceive. Sort of like a blessed surprise!

So, I share with you dear readers, please, do not give up; keep your faith, hold onto your dreams, and trust God. In fact, trust Him all the more, even when it does not look like it's going to happen for you. Just keep on trusting and believing.

Is it the Underlying Cause or a Symptom?

Jenei Ford

There was a time when I believed that happiness and fulfillment were contingent upon losing weight. In 2017, I gave birth to my second child, a beautiful baby boy, and like many mothers, I expected to feel a sense of love and joy every time I held my precious bundle of joy. However, my reality was far from that. I spent most of my days engulfed in despair, feeling isolated and deeply unhappy. Postpartum depression cast a dark cloud over my life, and to make matters worse, I was already diagnosed with PTSD, depression, and anxiety before becoming pregnant. It felt like I was merely existing in an abyss rather than truly living. I went from weighing 232 pounds before my pregnancy to 287 pounds afterward. I was knocking on the door of 300!

While some people might have taken this as a wake-up call and sought help to develop healthier habits, I remained trapped in my depression, using binge eating as a coping mechanism. I tried various fad diets and pills, but whenever I reached a weight loss goal, I would celebrate by binge eating again. The cycle of unhappiness persisted. In an attempt to portray a character of perfection to the outside world, I wore a mask. I became so encapsulated with the idea of being flawless that I lost sight of my true self. I denied my imperfections, and this mask became my shield to hide the fact that I was struggling with a binge-eating disorder, episodes of consuming large amounts of food in a short period of time coupled with the feelings of loss of control and a sense of distress or guilt afterward. It was my way of coping with the trauma, stress, and depressive moments, even during my time in the Air Force. I would starve myself to meet weight requirements and pass physical fitness tests, only to indulge in episodes of binge eating afterward.

It was a vicious cycle that continued for years, hidden beneath my carefully crafted mask. During this time, I firmly believed that losing weight would solve all my problems. My thoughts started with "Once I lose this weight, then..." or "If I lose this weight, then..." or "I need to lose this weight so I can..." I believed the cliché of "when you look good, you feel good." Yet, operating in these thoughts and beliefs, I soon discovered that weight gain was merely a symptom of my unhappiness.

In 2021, after continued failed attempts to lose weight, I made the decision to undergo bariatric surgery, hoping that it would be the solution to my binge-eating disorder. I viewed it as a physical restriction that would prevent me from indulging in my destructive eating habits. After the surgery, I experienced rapid weight loss, shedding 100 pounds in just eight months. It seemed like a great accomplishment, and I began to feel more confident and hopeful. But deep down, I still clung to my mask of perfection, questioning why I was still plagued by unhappiness. The tears and lack of patience with my children were constant reminders that there was something deeper within me that needed addressing. Why was I still sitting in these thoughts of anguish, hurt, and frustration? I had lost the weight. So, why was this mask still necessary? Why couldn't I see a way out of this abyss? How could I cope through these dark times when I was physically restricted from binge eating? The weight loss alone was not the answer.

In my search for a coping mechanism, I turned to alcohol. Unaware of transfer addiction, I traded one compulsive behavior for another. Alcohol became my new crutch; It was now the glue that held my mask in place. I was still perfect in the eyes of everyone around. My children appeared happy, and I excelled at work, but in 2022, everything came crashing down. I was arrested for drinking while intoxicated, and my mask shattered completely. I was exposed, and the dark abyss became my reality. I questioned my worth and believed that everyone would be better off without me. In this moment, the weight of disappointment and shame was extremely unbearable and had far outweighed any amount of physical weight lost previously. Amidst my struggles with alcoholism, migraines, and mental health challenges, I was forced to resign from work and sell my house. I had hit rock bottom and the question "What do I have left to offer on earth?" haunted my thoughts every day until the only answer that made sense at the time was "Nothing."

The bottle of depression medication on my nightstand seemed like the only way out. However, a small movement from my 5-year-old son, who was sleeping beside me, snapped me out of my trance. In that moment, as the tears flooded my eyes, I made the decision to hold onto him and never let go. It was then that I realized I had been focusing on the surface-level symptoms rather than addressing the underlying causes of my unhappiness. I had been wearing a mask, hiding behind a facade of perfection, instead of facing the truth. Through faith and acceptance, I began to understand that true transformation can only occur when we address the root cause rather than merely treating the symptoms. As an Air Force combat veteran and military sexual assault survivor, I embraced my purpose as a beacon of hope, resilience, and transformation. My children became my saving grace, and I found strength in overcoming the storms of trauma, mental health challenges, and alcoholism. It was through

God's grace and mercy that I emerged from the abyss, with a renewed faith in the beauty that life has to offer.

Even though I've lost 130 pounds, I learned that we could worsen our healing journey by putting a band-aid over a wound that actually requires stitches. It is through a journey of self-discovery and self-acceptance that we must be willing to unmask those negative thoughts or beliefs, accept our imperfections, and transform into that most invaluable person we were uniquely designed to be in this world.

Surviving One of the Darkest Parts of My Life

Sherry Landrum

If you've ever wondered if it is possible to heal and rebuild your life after surviving domestic violence, I am here to reassure you that you are an overcomer and are more than capable of doing just that.

I wanted to touch briefly on a small portion of my personal story. I was married to whom I thought was the love of my life, we had one child, and in my seven months of pregnancy with our second child, my husband abused me until I was almost unrecognizable. I had my child at 7 ½ months in utero. He faced several complications but by God's grace, survived and is with us today.

After being released from the hospital, it was then I decided to muster up the courage to leave. Divorce wasn't something that was in the cards for me as I grew up in a Christian home and it was against our beliefs. When I decided to leave, it became clear to me I would have the fight of my life on my hands. A rather ugly and long (seven years) custody battle was brewing, and much to my surprise, I lost that battle to my abuser. Fast forward a few years later and my abuser was found guilty of three counts of capital murder (again a domestic situation) and sentenced to life in prison. Our children were given to his parents for adoption. Imagine not being able to see your children for 13 years!

I know you're questioning *how*, but I don't want to steer you from the real reason we are here, which is for me to tell you what you are capable of. Domestic abuse can leave you with a lot of challenges

70

to face. The emotional trauma afterwards can leave us overwhelmed, which can lead to anxiety, depression, and low self-esteem. It can also leave a financial strain and cause social isolation, legal complications, concerns for safety, housing insecurity, and child custody issues. I have experienced all the above but let me address how I overcame those obstacles and how I know you can as well.

A lot of lessons were learned throughout the course of my journey to rebuilding my life again. I read a lot of self-help books, set boundaries (which is important), went for walks to clear my mind, and started a self-care routine. One key thing I did after all these years was seek professional counseling. Your friends and family are always good to talk with, but there is nothing better than someone who doesn't know you at all, and you are just laying it all out there for them to dissect with you, and help you reclaim your personal autonomy and rebuild a life free from violence. Affirmations were very key for me as well. Some of the things I remembered to say to myself as I looked in the mirror were,

- *Girl, you are enough, you are royalty and should be treated as such.*
- *You are worthy. You are loved. You are strong. You are beautiful.*
- *I persevere. I am relentless. I keep going.*
- *Today is a new beginning of whatever I want.*

My friend, it takes courage to leave an abusive situation. The challenges that come with that can be overwhelming. The thought of starting over, doing things on your own, and finding love again, it's overwhelming; it's literally facing the unknown. But you know what I do know? You are courageous enough to do so. The amount of strength and courage it takes in this decisive moment marks the beginning of the journey toward healing and empowerment!

I am encouraging you to refer to yourself as a survivor, not a victim. When you are resilient enough to survive this, you are changing the trajectory of your life. I had to start completely over with my life, and while the road wasn't easy, it was well worth it! I love myself again, have a great relationship with the Lord, met and married my best friend who is so amazing, restored my relationship with my older two children, and blessed by God with two more children! I now own my own business with my husband and life is simply sweet.

I want you to know that you will not only overcome these challenges, but you will grow emotionally, fostering a newfound sense of self. Make empowered choices by making positive changes for your well-being, whether it be pursuing education, career opportunities or healthier relationships. You will become an advocate either within your community or through support organizations, contributing to the awareness and prevention of domestic violence. You will also break generational patterns by causing a ripple effect, breaking the cycle of abuse and inspiring positive change for future generations.

You are resilient. You are capable and able to recover quickly from life's adversities. It is important to seek support, prioritize self-care, and embark on a path toward healing and empowerment, and in this, I pray you find inspiration and strength through your own challenges and experiences.

God will take what is broken, put it together again and make it better than it was before!

I Got Up

Audrey D. Mitchell

October 7, 2021, will forever be etched in my mind. I still remember the numbness, the tightening of my chest, the pain in my heart, and the doubt that took over my body. I received a phone call that the person I was committed to spending the rest of my life with was found deceased. This one event rocked me to my core. My world briefly stopped. Everything I believed in was challenged in one second, which felt like an eternity.

How was I to move on? How was I to live after everything we prayed and planned for was now suddenly gone? I lost my confidant. I lost my safe place where I could let my guard down and be vulnerable without judgment. That space doesn't come easy for me. I couldn't afford to give my trust and space within my inner circle to just anybody. My circle was (is) tight and very small. I am a strong Black woman who fights and helps others who can't fight for themselves. I am the shoulder people come and cry on and the advice-giver people seek when they are at their worst. Therefore, I have to be strong. But strong women need support, too, and on October 7, 2021, I had lost mine.

What now?

Honestly, I felt like God betrayed me. I felt alone and not good enough. My people rallied around me and just as people do, they asked the "appropriate" questions. What happened? I am so sorry,

73

how are you feeling? You guys were together for so long, what now? However, every time someone said something, it drew me right back into reliving the loss, getting angry, and even questioning my faith. Everyone had advice on what I should do, how I should feel, and they meant well. The week leading up to the funeral, one question kept coming to me: *Do you believe Me?* After every conversation with someone that usually involved me reliving what was lost, I kept hearing, "Do you believe Me?"

I had a choice to make. I saw it so clear. I could choose to stay and wallow in my loss, or I could choose to GET UP and STAND on the Word of God. If I truly believed in God like I professed to for so many years, then now was the time to put my faith to work and take Him at His Word.

How???

First, I had to get out of my head and stop listening to everyone's "advice." This meant I did NOT always answer the phone when my people called, and no matter what, I got out of bed. I GOT UP! Every day, no matter what, I GOT UP. I moved even when it felt like my heart was shattering into a million pieces. Even when I could not breathe and felt like my legs were going to fail me, I GOT UP! I allowed myself to feel but not dwell.

Before October 7, 2021, I went to the gym at 4 am and then did my morning devotional before work. Before October 7, 2021, I investigated complaints for the local NAACP branch and helped resolve injustices. I was an active member in the community, and that's what I was after the funeral. It was hard. I did not *feel* like it, but I made up my mind: I was NOT staying in grief, doubt, depression, fear, and sadness any longer. I acknowledged the areas where I doubted, questioned, and fell short. I dug deeper in the Word and studied scriptures that pertained to those areas. I searched out sermons, books, and songs that fed my spirit. I knew the Word before, and I had a relationship with God, but this was different. I was vehemently and consistently seeking after God, determined that I was not going to get stuck in the "wilderness." God's promises are for me, too. I did not care what my current circumstances looked like. I did not care how empty I felt sometimes. I was determined to have what God said was mine. When those feelings of regret and disappointments came up, I learned that I have the power to cast them down. So, I crafted a playlist of songs, affirmations, and scriptures and repeated those until those "feelings" disappeared. I personalized my go-to scriptures with my name so I knew God was talking to me! I still do! Why? I learned that words create. What you hear, you will eventually say. Using the right words consistently will shift your current mood and your mindset. When your mindset is properly aligned, your entire situation will shift in the direction you are believing, praying, and hoping for! The same is true for the opposite. So, watch what you say.

I also allowed God to heal the hurt by acknowledging what I was mourning. The obvious, I missed him. The not so obvious was I was mourning my plans. I spent 5 ½ years with my best friend planning, growing, encouraging, protecting, and supporting each other. Then in a blink of an eye, nothing. I was angry, and I was afraid. I knew I could not stay here and have the life God promised. The more I studied, I mean really studied the Word, it went from information to revelation. This was a faith fight. My children, grandchildren, family, and future depended on me getting this right. I wanted God's promises, so I was focused on doing it God's way.

My circumstances were real, but God's Word is TRUTH. If I didn't Get Up in 2021 and push past my circumstances, I wouldn't have found a peace that only comes from God. Now I am positioned and ready for opportunities and relationships that God ordained just for me.

Yes, October 7, 2021, will forever be etched in my mind but today for different reasons. Now, it motivates me to pursue everything God promised me. It reminds me that I AM Worthy!

I Am More than Enough

Donnetta Moore

Tests and trials come to make you strong. Phil. 4:13 says I can do all things through Christ that strengthens me. I AM Worthy of everything that God has given me. I AM Worthy of everything God has in store for me!

What do you do when you are up for a promotion and your character is being assassinated, when you are being lied on, when your reputation is being destroyed in public, when your name is being slandered, when you are experiencing attacks on every side? What do you do when your back is against the wall, and it looks as if it's over? What do you do when you know this is your season and something you have worked and prayed for is staring you in your face and is slipping from your grasps? Whenever you are going through a storm, you must find scriptures that will resonate with what you are dealing with. I had to block all distractions the naysayers and doubters threw my way.

For I know the thoughts that I think toward you saith the Lord thoughts of peace and not of evil to give you an expected end.
Jeremiah 29:11

I had to go to God for myself. I had to cry out to God and ask God how long would I have to endure these attacks. I had to continue to smile and go to work with the same people who were backbiting and speaking all manners of evil against me. God had to hide me in plain sight. They could see me, but they couldn't touch me. I had to steal away in my secret place where I could get naked before God, telling him my innermost longings and reminding him of his promises every step of the way. God is a man who cannot lie; if he said it in his word, he would bring it to pass. I had to search the scriptures that answered my prayers. The battle was too great for me to fight alone. I cried out to God, asking him to plead my cause, O LORD, with them that strive with me: fight against them that fight against me. Psalms 35:1 God did just what he said in his word!

No matter the attack, I held my peace and let God fight, for this battle was too much for me to handle! God will get in the battle with you and give you victory. All you have to do is put your trust totally in him, seek his face, tell him all about it, and watch God change things.

I knew greater was coming. I allowed God to take me to that higher place in him. No matter how your situation looks, continue to keep your eyes on God, stay in prayer, and watch God turn that situation around. In the secret place is where you set the atmosphere so God can talk to you and deal with you right where you are. When you let go and let God have his way, that's when he shows up on the scene and give you the victory. Everything you need is in the word of God; decree and declare what the scripture says and put God in remembrance of his word. Continue to praise and worship him through it all, and once he gives you what you ask for, continue to thank him for answering your prayers. What is impossible with man is possible with God.

Instead of giving up hope in what appeared to be a hopeless situation, I persevered and pushed passed the dirty looks, the doubters, the naysayers, being outcast, setbacks, and obstacles. I held firm to the word of God, I continued to pray, and I recited Psalm 91, Psalm 35, and Psalm 23 daily.

On December 12, 2023, I was officially promoted to principal.

Every answer to your circumstances or problems is in the word of God. How do you know God answers your prayers? Jeremiah 33:3: *Call unto me, and I will answer thee and show thee great and mighty things.*

Your faith must match whatever you are believing God for. Search the scriptures to give you the answers you need. You are coming into a season of no more, no more waiting, no more lack, no more closed doors, no more struggle, no more putting up with people who serve no purpose in your life, no more delays. I decree and declare you are getting ready for a shift of a supernatural release in the name of Jesus. The divine season of no more is going to break every chain, loose every stronghold, remove every hindrance, remove every generational curse, remove every ungodly soul tie, remove toxins, and remove all roadblocks, setbacks and blockages.

In the midst of it all, God allowed me to bend, but he didn't let me break. You are about to **POP** as you were **P**repared **O**n **P**urpose. Everything you went through was necessary for your growth and development in Christ Jesus. No matter what I went through, no matter what situations arose, no matter what difficulties I endured or was faced with, I never lost my hope, I never lost my joy, I never lost my faith, and I never lost my praise. Praise confuses the enemy. What are you waiting on to praise God? If God walked up to you right now and told you your praise is going to give you what you been asking him for, how would you respond? When praises go up, blessings come down. What are you waiting on to praise God? I will bless the Lord at all times; his praises shall continually be in mouth.

I will continue to learn from my experiences and strive to become the best version of me. I am excited about the woman that I'm becoming because I fought to become her, she is me! **I AM MORE THAN ENOUGH!**

Reclaiming Your Worth and Greatness

Sharrarne Morton

In a world that often seeks to diminish the worth of Black women, it is so very important to remind ourselves of our value and dignity. Despite facing harsh inequalities and historical injustices, as well as the constant feeling that we're just not good enough, Black women possess an innate worthiness that just cannot be diminished.

Resilience and Strength Equals Worthiness

Since the beginning of time, Black women have demonstrated remarkable resilience and strength in the face of severe and uninterrupted adversity. From the struggles of slavery to the civil rights movement and beyond, Black women have been at the forefront of social change and progress. Our ability to persevere in the face of overwhelming challenges from within and outside our race speaks to our strength and resilience.

The Color of Worthiness

Black women have made significant contributions to art, literature, music, science, politics, and every other facet of society. We have left a mark on history because of our creativity, intellect, and innovation that has enriched the world in countless ways, emphasizing our undeniable value and importance.

I Am Worthy

Self-Care

In a society that often perpetuates harmful stereotypes and standards of beauty, it is crucial for Black women to prioritize self-love and self-care in order to feel worthy. Embracing our hair no matter its texture, celebrating our curves, and affirming our beauty in all its forms are acts of self-care and love in a world that seeks to dictate our worth based on narrow standards of beauty.

Bonds and Sisterhood

Black women have a long tradition of supporting and uplifting one another through community and sisterhood. Whether through organizations, churches, or social networks, we have created spaces where we can share our joys, pains, and triumphs. Building strong bonds of sisterhood has always fostered a sense of belonging and solidarity among us, reminding us that we are never alone in our journey toward self-worth.

Reclaiming Our Narratives

Black women are often subjected to barriers such as dangerous stereotypes that portray us as angry and aggressive. Challenging these stereotypes and reclaiming our narratives is an essential part of affirming our worth. By refusing to be defined by stereotypes, we assert our dignity and self-worth.

Black women have been and always will be the embodiment of resilience, strength, and beauty. Our mere existence enriches the world and contributes to the tapestry of human experience. By embracing our worthiness, we empower ourselves to live authentically and unapologetically even in a society that seeks to diminish us. We are wonderfully worthy—every day and in every way.

I Have RA, but RA Does NOT Have Me
Ashley Nicole

Introduction: Embracing Faith Amidst Challenges

"For I know the plans I have for you," declares the Lord, "plans to prosper you and not to harm you, plans to give you hope and a future." ~Jeremiah 29:11

But what happens when hope and the future are challenged?

I'll tell you what happens…YOU LEARN TO FIGHT!

The Onset of Rheumatoid Arthritis: A Battle Begins

My rheumatoid arthritis (RA) symptoms began at 21, starting with pain and stiffness in my hands. I remember the fear overtaking vividly.

One morning, in my University of North Alabama dorm, I experienced a full-body flare. I was in shock and completely puzzled. Showering, pain filled. Brushing my teeth, excruciating. Combing my hair, complete agony. I felt like I was in a nightmare where buttoning and zipping my clothes became foreign to my joints. What was going on with my body? I was living a 24/7 nightmare, and without proper insurance, it took six years to learn my diagnosis.

A Journey of Pain and Perseverance

Flare-ups often left my hands swollen and painful, hindering basic tasks like cooking and cleaning. Unbeknownst to me, certain lifestyle habits were exacerbating these flare-ups. My rheumatologist focused on medications, overlooking the potential benefits of nutrition, hydration, and exercise.

I was 27 and had already endured severe, irreversible joint damage. Then to my surprise, during my treatment, I was diagnosed with lupus, complicating my health further and creating more uncertainty about my future. And divorce came a few years later. I remember struggling to find myself worthy of overcoming this illness and achieving success.

Finding My Identity: The Turning Point

In 2019 after nearly 13 years of marriage, a turning point occurred. It was my 36th birthday, and as a newly single woman, I pondered, *Who is Ashley Nicole?* Growing up in a church-centered family instilled a strong foundation of faith in me, shaping the woman I am today. Mentorship and faith were my backbone through the adversities of adult life, from my RA and lupus diagnoses to navigating career shifts and life post-divorce. I had to hold on to every bit of strength that God placed within me. Who did I want to be now though?

A New Beginning: God-fidence and RA Warrior Fitness

Clarity emerged in January 2020.

During a period of fasting and praying, I attended a vision board event named "God-fidence." It was here that I shared my dream of

84

using my certifications to aid women with RA and autoimmune conditions.

Then a sermon and a moment of struggle during a fitness class led to a divine revelation: "RA Warrior Fitness." I quickly established my business, building a website and setting up a virtual program platform. Even the onset of the pandemic in March 2020 didn't halt my plans; I launched RA Warrior Fitness amidst being furloughed and later laid off from my full-time job.

Triumph Over Adversity: Building RA Warrior Fitness

And while the global pandemic's challenges hit, I was equipped to create a business empowering women facing similar struggles. My faith and my journey had affirmed my worthiness and transformed my pain into purpose, profit, and power.

I went from 220 pounds to a healthy 140. Despite discouragement from a close confidant about my aspirations to become a certified personal trainer, I pursued my passion. Not only did I become a trainer, but I also specialized in fitness nutrition, strength training, and endurance training, which qualified me as a master trainer.

Conclusion: A Journey of Empowerment and Worthiness

Since its inception, RA Warrior Fitness has transformed the lives of over 275 women globally. Our mission is to empower women with autoimmune diseases to alleviate joint discomfort and boost energy through faith, food, and fitness. I now walk firmly in my purpose.

My journey as a business owner, natural bodybuilding pro, and contributor to publications like *Women's Health Magazine* continues to inspire others. RA may be a part of my life, but it does not define me. I am, unequivocally, WORTHY!

The Strength of Letting Go
Dr. Dawn Sheree Paramore

"You never know how strong you are until being strong is the only choice you have."
Bob Marley

Trauma

Monday, February 11, 2013, was no ordinary day. It was the very moment that prematurely birthed my career as a psychotherapist specializing in trauma. During that time, I was a clinical intern still working on my master's degree in clinical mental health when I met a young woman seeking assistance involved in an international stalking case who appeared on Jim Walsh's *America's Most Wanted*.

The work I did was meaningful; however, despite positive strides, both myself and this young woman were aware of the probability that her life could end tragically. Regardless of the possible reality, we were both making productive traction in therapy, and she trusted me as a student with a severe case of imposter syndrome, as I did not think I was good enough to work with her with the complications of her case.

Our last encounter left us both anxious as she informed me that she was summoned to appear in court for a child support case. Knowing the complexities, I advised her not to go for safety concerns but to contact victim advocates. She agreed, disclosing alternative plans to remain home, but assured me she would follow up for a subsequent session. That incident was the first time I trusted my instincts without evidence supporting the decision.

Despite what we agreed that morning, she decided to attend the hearing at the courthouse. She made a pit stop before arriving at her destination, dropping off a card to thank me for all I had done to assist her and her family. The act alone was out of character, as she had never done such a thing before, yet I was grateful for her act of gratitude. In the handwritten card, she reminded me that it was hard to find a therapist due to the various difficulties involved with her case, but she made a point of providing the sweetest letter of encouragement. She requested that I stay hungry for the love of helping people and never doubt my abilities and capacity to serve others.

After dropping the card off, she continued her travels to the courthouse, arriving at her destination with her friend. Shortly upon entering the building, her ex-father-in-law opened fire in the lobby of the courthouse, killing her and the friend who accompanied her before turning the gun on himself. The horrifying event left three people dead, including the shooter, and two others injured. Other clinicians saw the news and pulled me aside, informing me of this tragedy. I did not believe them, so I grabbed the phone to contact her, but she did not answer. All I had remaining was the card she dropped off earlier that day. It took years before I could drive past that courthouse or even forgive myself for not doing a better job of talking her out of the last-minute decision to appear in court.

A few years later, several witnesses and survivors testified, including myself, to provide their accounts of the events and the circumstances surrounding the shooting. These testimonies played a crucial role in establishing the facts of the case and helping the court understand the sequence of events that led to the shooting. As a result, my clinical recordings, as required as a clinical intern, were utilized to seek justice on her behalf, even allowing her voice to be played while I was testifying.

Imposter Syndrome

The 2013 Delaware Courthouse Shooting served as a sad reminder of the importance of addressing not only the physical safety of court facilities but also the emotional and psychological toll that protracted legal battles can take on those involved. This shocking incident highlighted the critical security issue in courthouses and the need for improved safety measures to protect employees and visitors. As for me, it was an awful reminder of survivor's guilt and imposter syndrome, constantly questioning if my work was "good enough" to protect her or wondering if I had failed this woman.

I was fortunate to engage in counseling to assist with the trauma I experienced, but I had to learn to be patient and to love myself while embracing the hurt. Forgiveness is not easy. The most challenging person I had to forgive that day was myself. Now, I advocate for trauma-informed care, being a therapeutic voice for those who are broken but desire the opportunity to be renewed and restored. I have also learned to trust my gut, reminding myself I am worthy and good enough.

Forgiveness

Forgiveness is profoundly important in our lives as it is a powerful catalyst for healing and personal growth. When we forgive, we release ourselves from the heavy burden of anger, resentment, and pain that can consume us from the shackles of bitterness. Ultimately, forgiveness is a gift we give ourselves, allowing us to embrace the nectar of a more harmonious and fulfilling life. Here are some general steps you can consider when working toward forgiveness:

1. Acknowledge Your Feelings
2. Understand the Impact
3. Practice Self-Compassion
4. Engage in Empathy / Perspective-Talking
5. Let Go of Resentment
6. Seek a Trained Professional
7. Be Honest about Your Feelings
8. Practice Patience
9. Focus on Healing
10. Give Permission to Receive Unconditional Love

To the resilient soul reading this chapter who has faced adversity and triumphed over the darkest of storms, your strength is immeasurable, and your courage is inspiring. Despite your pain, you have shown incredible resilience and fortitude by just showing up, making a decision, and reading this book. Your past does not define you, nor does your trauma. Remember that healing is a journey with every step taken toward recovery, which is a testament to your unwavering spirit. May each day bring you closer to peace, finding strength and hope in the light within you. As best said by Bob Marley, "You never know how strong you are until being strong is the only choice you have." You got this!

Bayron Watts, You Are Not Taking My Lunch! Not Today! Never Again!

Terolyn Phinsee

I was 12 years old, thin, tall for my age, and intimidated by the big man-sized 14-year-old Bayron Watts as he stood in front of me, blocking me from my way to school.

I had woke up late that morning—no time for breakfast of biscuits and honey. I threw on my clothes, washed my face, brushed my teeth, took my night scarf off, and looked myself in the mirror.

"I am not afraid, Bayron Watts."

Needless to say, my words had always proven to have more courage than I demonstrated. I checked my newly pressed hair, put on my jacket, grabbed my new books, ran through the kitchen to grab the delicious lunch that my aunt Cille, Dolomite's Press N'Curl Queen, made for me, and whisked hurriedly out the door to catch up with my friends so we could walk to school together.

It was the second day of the new school year. I was excited to return this day because I did not see Bayron on the first day of school. I had hoped that he would not be returning to my school, and I would not have to give him my lunch as I had for weeks before summer break.

My friends Juanita, Hattie, and I laughed and giggled contagiously as we shared stories about our summer activities, which included visits home to see my mom and siblings. Our conversations came to an abrupt end when we saw the image of Bayron Watts heading toward us. Juanita and Hattie looked at me and simultaneously said, "Just hurry pass him."

Fear consumed me, and I froze in my tracks. It seemed that Bayron had grown even bigger than the year before; he was a giant. I tucked my books under my left arm and squeezed my brown bagged lunch tightly in my right hand.

Bayron streamlined straight to me; it was like he saw no one else there. "Louise," he demanded, "give me your lunch with your boney self."

I looked down at the sidewalk as he proceeded to raise his hand to snatch my lunch from my hand. Something rose up within me, and without thinking, I yelled, "Bayron Watts, you are not taking my lunch! Not today! Never again!" I dropped my books and my coveted lunch, and began swinging my arms, grabbing his face, scratching him wildly, jumping up on him and knocking him to the ground. I kept beating him in the head until my friends Juanita and Hattie, and other students pulled me off of him. Bayron's parents took him to the hospital for the injuries he sustained. Needless to say, I never had another problem with Bayron Watts. That was the day that I realized that my courage in life had to be bigger than my fears and that there would be more Bayron Watts in my life that I would have to stand up to without fear.

The next Bayron Watts experience came eleven years later. As newlyweds, William and I were stationed in Paris, France, thousands of miles away from my family. I was pregnant with our third child while William was staying out late, drinking with his army buddies and doing other unsavory things. When he'd returned intoxicated, he began hitting me. It took courage to resist fighting him to avoid harming the baby and scaring my one- and two-year-old babies. I was a faithful wife and good mother. Realizing that abuse and dysfunction was not God's will for me and my children, I began saving my military spouse allotments and confided in a wonderful Godly woman; she was our military housing landlord.

On a cold Monday morning, William left for duty, and I grabbed our coats, food, suitcases, and the allotment money I'd saved, and my landlord took me to the airport where I boarded a plane with my two precious babies and returned to the United States where I hid with my children. William returned to our military home and found that I had left. Our landlord never said a word, and I never saw him again.

I never looked back.

There will be times when your Bayron Watts experiences will cause you to make flight instead of fight, especially if fighting will cause harm to you or someone you love. Remember that a fight doesn't have to be physical. Sometimes, the fight is just putting your foot down and leaving a Bayron Watts and not giving up your lunch.

Within ten years, I remarried to wonderful, caring man. Newly relocated to Long Beach, California, I would go on to experience another Bayron Watts experience, but this time in the workplace as one of the first African American women in nursing with the US government. The Jim Crow mindset was not as prevalent in Los Angeles, but it was still very real. I refused to take "No" as an answer for my request to go to nursing school and take the exam. The Nursing Board wasn't going to take my lunch. I refused to take 'No' for an answer when my husband and I moved my family from the rough neighborhoods to a predominantly white neighborhood.

Facing the Bayron Watts experiences in my life without fear has allowed me to purchase and hold onto an extensive amount of real estate, start my own specialty meat company, own my own independent senior living facility, and raise four amazing children.

Who and what are your Bayron Watts? An abusive spouse, a job that is holding you back, or poor past choices? Have self-respect. Stand up for yourself. Refuse to live in dysfunction. God is always with us. Hold your head up. Don't look back. Even if you have to do it afraid and alone. Don't allow anything or anyone to take what God has for you. Stop giving away your lunch.

Beyond Betrayal, Hurt, and Pain
Zhelinrentice Scott

All through my life, I have been told what I could and should do. I was really driven and undeterred in my life until I got married. I married my college sweetheart in 2002, and we had our daughter a year later in 2003. We were living a great life until I was diagnosed with manic depression. Before I was diagnosed with manic depression, I was an honors intern for the FBI, a candidate for a master's degree in public policy from the University of Michigan Ann Arbor, and an alumnae of the Massachusetts Institute of Technology.

Manic depression plus betrayal threw me into a tailspin. Manic Depression caused doctors and my ex-husband to gang up on me. I did not have the support that I desired, and I could not articulate what I needed effectively. In my frustration, and as the answer, I filed for divorce. I divorced my daughter's father, and as my life progressed, I found myself a victim of parental alienation, poverty, and mental illness.

Because my divorce was not amicable and I did not share with my family details of what I was going through, I really felt betrayed. I stayed in Michigan from 2002 to 2014 because I did not trust my family, and I was determined to make it on my own.

As I was determined to find my road to recovery from a broken marriage and manic depression, I desperately wanted to get back on the path of the life that I had envisioned as a child. I continued therapy in search of answers. I was in therapy, and in my mind, I wanted someone to give me the answers to my problems so that I could get a good job and thrive.

So, as I was in a therapy appointment, this woman looked at me, knowing my story of having two degrees from MIT and a master's from the University of Michigan Ann Arbor, and told me to go get a job at Target as a cashier. I was stunned. I was completely disappointed in her advice, and at that moment, I knew that it was just me and God. When she gave me the advice to just aim as low as I possibly could to live, I then started searching for more answers. There are two places that I turned for answers. The first is the Bible, and the second is myself.

When I hit rock bottom, I began to hold on to scriptures like Revelations 21 and 22. These two scriptures talk about how heaven and the New Jerusalem will look. In Revelation Chapter 21, there is a detailed description of how Heaven looks. In Revelation 22, there is a description of the Throne of God and the flora and fauna surrounding his eternal seat of authority. It is this description that gave me the hope and faith that I needed at my lowest moment emotionally and financially. In Revelation 22:2 it states, "In the midst of the street of it, and on either side of the river, was there the tree of life, which bore twelve manner of fruits, and yielded her fruit every month: and the leaves of the tree were for the healing of the nations."

This scripture encouraged my soul, and it made me understand that I am worthy to continue walking this path in spite of my mistakes, hurt, and pain. This scripture more importantly showed me how Heaven IS a place of healing. When you have been betrayed, under-appreciated, cast aside, and forgotten as much as we as Black women are and as much as I have, it was comforting and a game-changer for me. This scripture made me understand three things about healing:

- Healing will take time. This tree near the Throne of God will give leaves for the healing of the nations for ETERNITY. God takes my hurt and pain seriously. So seriously that he already has a healing regime ready for me and those who love him in heaven.

- You don't have to Heal on Your OWN. I am worthy of God's healing touch and grace. I am so comforted by the revelation that God's LOVE is so eternal that he has a plan for the disappointments that I have faced in this life.

- I am Worthy. Before I was a twinkle in my parents' eyes, John on the Island of Patmos wrote a book dictated to him by God. This book is The Book of Revelation of Jesus Christ. Jesus Christ died on the cross for my sins. He died a horrible death, an infinite sacrifice for mankind's sin. Jesus Christ died for my sin. This realization that God created me with every single need met and scenario covered helped me to rededicate my life to walking exclusively by faith. No matter what challenges come my way, I know that I am worthy to keep pushing.

What Is on the Other Side of Fear?
Shermeaka Settles

During my childhood, I was often timid and shy. My peers would frequently tease and mock me. Despite this, I was passionate about education and consistently excelled academically. My teachers believed that I would go on to achieve great success and recognition. However, I constantly felt powerless to defend myself against the cruelty of others. I allowed the fear of judgment to control me. Unfortunately, this fear persisted throughout my school years and eventually led me to drop out of high school. It's disheartening to think that I allowed the fear of what others thought to deprive me of an education.

The fear of people's opinions continued to dominate my life. I missed out on numerous career opportunities because I was afraid of how my ideas would be received. I even passed on record deals and music opportunities because I allowed fear to diminish my confidence. Deep down, I knew I possessed the skills and qualifications to achieve anything I desired. I was well aware of my exceptional singing voice. Interestingly, it was often the areas from which fear drove me away that were closely linked to my purpose. It wasn't just about knowing my potential; it was about summoning the courage within me to overcome fear and confront whatever challenges lay ahead. Our purpose in life often lies on the other side of our anxieties and fears.

I had to endure significant losses and missed opportunities before I finally confronted the fear of how others perceived me. The passage of time, life experiences, and personal setbacks ultimately ignited a newfound boldness within me. I refuse to allow the fear of people to hinder my progress any longer. Today, I have performed and ministered on numerous platforms. I have also held management positions where I have guided and nurtured the careers of others. None of these accomplishments would have been possible if I hadn't made the decision to embrace boldness.

I am determined to no longer live a life burdened by fear and anxiety.

I Am Enough
Sharee Williams

Who I am doesn't really matter. But why I am is the real question. I have faced many challenges and have overcome them with strength and courage. I was told I would be on welfare, have a bunch of children, and not know who the fathers—this from people who said they loved me. I listened to that for years and allowed it to keep me in bondage, feeling worthless and unworthy.

One day, I had enough of me and began to talk to God and asked him, "Who am I? *Why* am I?"

He showed me a glimpse of how he saw me. He told me I was fearfully and wonderfully made, that he knew me before I was formed in my mother's womb, that he had a plan for me that was good not evil but had an expected end. Through life's ups and downs, ins and outs, bad decisions, and trials, God had his hand on me, and he didn't let any of it to kill me.

Through adversity, I have learned to navigate in today's world, not only as a woman but as an individual. The first thing I needed to learn was how to navigate as an individual. Then, I had to learn how to navigate myself as a woman; I had to learn how to be okay being me no matter how difficult that might had been. I had to learn that I mattered even if it was to no one but myself.

I had to learn to love myself.

It may sound corny, but I have conversations with myself. (I am smart, I am beautiful, and yes. I am enough.). At first, yes, it sounded weird, but I said these words long enough that it that they got down in my spirit, and I began to believe it for myself. I began to hold my head up, stand tall, and believe in me.

I do have a lot of children—ten to be exact, six boys and four girls. Of the four girls, two were adopted and one daughter passed away.

Oh, and I was on welfare as well.

Many times, life doesn't pan out the way YOU plan, but it always turns out the way God plans it. Life can and will knock you flat on your back, and it will seem as though you have lost the battle. None of what I had lived was originally planned by me for my life. It is a true statement that a good man/woman falls seven times, and that it's not in the fall but in the getting back up that's important. Yes, I had to get back up each time I fell. Each time I fell, there was a new lesson that I needed to learn. In my falling, I learned that I had talents, dreams, and visions and that they were very unique. They were my very own dreams and visions that God had given me, but if I had never had the adversity, I would have never known that I was enough.

Because I realized that I am enough, I am a wife of more than thirty years, the founder of a non-profit (3Phases of Becoming a Woman), and the CEO of Alppha's Homecare and Holistic Services.

YOU ARE ENOUGH!

Trust God Always
Katrenia Wright

I am worthy simply because God said so! Throughout my life, I have been faced with challenges that have required me to rely solely on my faith in God. Now some folks may say, "Here she goes, getting all religious on us." However, let me tell you that as a woman who was adopted at only six months old after my birth mother died, I have faced more challenges than I believe the law should allow. As a young child, I did not feel as though I fit in simply because my skin was much browner than that of all my first cousins. I'm telling you that every single one of my female cousins on both sides of my family are all light skinned. Even after being told that I was beautiful, I felt less than, and I also felt unwanted! See, my birth mother, unfortunately, was an alcoholic, or at least that's the story that I was told, and she died of cirrhosis of the liver. In my mind, although I had loving parents who showed me nothing but love, I could not, for the life of me, understand why I wasn't enough to stop my mother from drinking herself to death.

As I grew older, feeling like an only child because both my brothers were much older, I began to feel beyond blessed to know that there were two people whose hearts were so big that they went to New York City from Flint, Michigan, to pick up this little six-month-old baby girl to adopt her and raise her as their own. That baby girl was me! What an incredible blessing it is to have parents love you when they did not birth you. In time, I grew to learn that I was extremely special.

Now as time would go on and I grew up, I realized that my mother was stricter than a drill sergeant. At least my thoughts of what a drill sergeant was like because growing up I couldn't do hardly anything but go down the street and play with my friend Greta. Between the two of us, Greta and I had every piece of anything that was made for Barbie. We had an unbelievable amount of Barbie dolls, cars, mansions, and accessories; you name it, we had it! Not only did we play together daily, but from time to time, we were allowed to have sleepovers at each other's houses. As kids, we were inseparable. That may be why after 53 years of friendship, we are still friends and have a vacation planned together this summer.

Anyway, while I couldn't do half of what the other kids in my neighborhood could do, my mother, in particular, made sure that I learned how to do everything under the sun, from doing laundry, cooking, and cleaning to learning how to bowl, swim, dance, judo, play the piano, and study my Bible. Youth Fellowship every Friday and Sunday school every week at Grace Emmanuel Baptist Church was a must. Religion, you could say, was merely instilled in me. My father, on the other hand, taught me how to fish, shoot pool, and ride a bicycle. Together, they both showed me phenomenal examples of what it looks like to be great people. My parents were married for 55 years before my dad passed away, and my mother lived another ten years and died in February 2019.

As an adult facing adulthood challenges, I quickly realized that the very religion that was instilled in me as a child is what I could rely on when I faced challenges. Prayer has been my key to overcoming life's obstacles. I always trust God to lead me on the path that I need to go. Having overcome being a single mother, marrying and divorcing three times, building a career from scratch, then walking away from it so that I could properly raise my children has been only some of the toughest battles and decisions in my life. I've additionally overcome a brief encounter with domestic violence twice, being raped, and instances of homelessness both with and without children. Through it all, I was blessed to buy my first home as a single mother of five in 1999. That purchase let me know that with prayer, dedication, determination, and commitment for greatness for both myself and my children will only lead to blessings and great outcomes.

Fast forward to today, and I can truly say that, as a woman with many stories of triumph, that life is not only about what you make it but, what you genuinely believe that you deserve. I know that as a woman of faith in God, I possess the ability to do anything that I set my mind to. I am worthy of all the blessings that God has bestowed upon me until my cup runneth over in abundance. What I can say about this thing called life is; it's not easy, and we all have ups and downs, yet God remains faithful to loving us. I'm a witness, and I personally believe that anyone can overcome anything if they just step into a shower; and ask God to wash their problems down the drain and renew them with the power of his mercy as the water cleanses their body, so shall God cleanse their hearts and minds. So, I say to you in this moment, you should know that you too are worthy, and you can do anything, and you will excel if you just believe in yourself and trust God.

Say it with me, *"I am worthy and beautiful. I can do all things through Christ that strengthens me, and I will never stop striving to be the very best that I can be. I don't owe anyone anything, and no one owes me anything; therefore, every day I will strive for greatness believing in my heart and knowing in my mind that I AM WORTHY!"*

I Am Worthy
Contributors

Tiffany Anthony (FB: tdearmon1) is a successful entrepreneur and spiritual leader who is committed to her community. Through her leadership (management in the mortgage field, tax preparation and business consultant), survivorship (Lupus), memberships, entrepreneurial skills, and achievements, she helps build positive and strong business relationships and educate others in these skills. Business website: goldrushfinancialandtaxservice.com

Dr. Shela M. Cameron is a spiritual and dedicated leader who is committed to her community (locally and abroad) and the military. Through her leadership (34 years active duty-Lieutenant Colonel) survivorship (breast cancer), memberships (Delta Sigma Theta Sorority, Inc. & Order of Eastern Star), entrepreneurship skills (CEO of Trusted Real Estate Investment

Opportunities and Camy's Treasures, MLO – mortgage loan officer, best-selling author), achievement (BS, MA, and PhD); she mentors, teaches, builds relationships and businesses, educates, and provides resource, knowledge and networks to promote opportunities for people. She enjoys traveling, meeting people, and loving the Lord. Website: www.dr-shelamcameron.com

Felicia Cox, aka "The IronDiva," (IG: irondivas | FB: Felicia Cox) is an IFBB PRO Bodybuilder. She has been competing in bodybuilding for over 18 years. She is a wife, mother, successful business owner, and fitness expert. Learn more about Felicia at the following online outlets:
Website: deejsfitnation.com

Shawn Cunningham is an award-winning television news anchor and talk show host. Shawn launched her own production venture called Empowered for Success. She is also the content creator/producer of several multiplatform shows, including the award-winning *The Shawn Cunningham Show.*

DC native Rev. Allison G. Daniels (IG: allisongdaniels) is an international award-winning bestselling author of 41+ books, co-author of 21 books, publisher, multi-visionary, and a recipient of the Presidential Lifetime Achievement Award. She holds a degree in business administration. Website: www.agdpublishingservices.com

Avis Dillard-Bullock (IG: speaklifecaffe) is a military retiree and chief operating officer at a multimillion-dollar company in Washington, DC. She has a bachelor's in business and a master's in divinity and is on Develop Africa's Board of Directors. She's a wife, mother, and Christian. Website: www.speaklifecaffe.com

Jenei Ford (IG: iamjenei) is an Air Force Combat Veteran and founder of Unmask & Transform LLC. Her passion is creating and facilitating holistic safe spaces worldwide, where individuals can bravely embrace their vulnerability for personal growth, healing, and radical transformation. Website: https://unmaskingtransformation.com/

Kristee Hall (IG: itscoachkristee) is a motivational influencer, mother, author, certified life coach, voiceover artist, model, actress, and federal grant professional. Known for her federal career, her passion lies in assisting women in the federal civilian sector, through FedChick LLC. Website: www.KristeeHall.com

An AMBASSADOR 4 CHRIST, Kimberly Jackson-Jones (IG: LMJesusFamous) is an author, artist, praise and worship leader, and interim pastor. A CEO and producer of film and music, Kimberly uses her gifts, talents, and resources to help EMPOWER communities and make JESUS famous. Website: www.LetzMakeJESUSFamous.com

Sherry Landrum (FB: sherry.l.green.9) is a woman of God, military wife, mother to 4, born-again Christian, successful entrepreneur, and advocate for women empowerment. A co-owner of Golden Agila LLC (financial/business consultant services), Sherry has been in the health and wellness industry for 15 plus years and is CRCR certified.

Dr. Amicitia Maloon-Gibson (FB: InspireLeadGrow Academy) is an executive leadership consultant whose passion and purpose is empowering others. She is the EmpowermentDoc™ who Inspires, Leads, and Grows others. A lifelong learner, she believes in giving to the next generation. Website: www.empowermentdoc.com

Dr. Dianna Maria is a #1 bestselling author and the recipient of the 2022 United Nations Woman of Distinction Award, the 2023 Presidential Lifetime Achievement Award, and the 2023 Innovator of the Year Award. She is a health and wellness accountability expert, successful entrepreneur, and pro motivational speaker. Website: www.myspaneeds.com

Marlena Martin (IG: woapageant) is the CEO of Woman of Achievement, an organization that recognizes women in the U.S. and internationally who have strong community platforms and are making a difference in public speaking, the arts, and self-development. Website: www.womanofachievement.com

Audrey Mitchell (IG: audreyd_mitchell | FB: audrey.mitchell.73) is an entrepreneur, educator, and advocate. She loves mentoring and motivating the next generation to use their voices to affect REAL change. One of her recent accomplishments is developing and teaching a collegiate course, "What I Do Matters...How?" Website: audreydmitchell.com

Delma Montanez is a certified life coach, co-author of nine books, and a Toastmasters speaker who is passionate about helping people turn aspirations into reality. She serves as a financial adviser for companies, such as Fidelity Investment and Merrill Lynch. Website: SheThinksRich.biz

Donnetta Moore (IG: Dmoore422) is a supportive, caring, creative, and inspiring motivational speaker whose smile and personality lights up a room. Donnetta is a god-fearing prayer warrior and intercessor used by God to Speak Life into anyone that she encounters.

Sharrarne Morton is a former television commentator for an ABC News affiliate in Washington, DC, and is currently a host on SiriusXM Radio. While commentating, Sharrarne also launched Morton Media where she coaches businesses on how to leverage the power of media to scale. Sharrarne knows the importance of giving back. In 2021, she founded Black Door Society, an organization that connects women of color to high net worth and high network opportunities. Sharrarne recently got the opportunity to launch her own organic skincare line in the U.S. and Dubai called Skin Deep Beauty.

Websites: www.sharrarnemorton.com, www.blackdoorsociety.org, www.skindeepbeautystore.com

---

Regina Nelson APRN, FNP-C, PMHNP-BC is a mother, grandmother, and businesswoman. Her motto is "If we don't go, who will?" Her love is providing psychiatric mental health care. As a minister of the gospel with a servant's heart, she provides assistance and support through her nonprofit Food for Life and the food bank of Northwest Indiana. She sat on the board of Brother Keepers in Gary, Indiana. Her experience includes healthcare provider, consultant, coach, mentor, advocate, and co-author. Her favorite saying is "Wear this world like a loose garment, and live life with no regrets."

Dedicated fitness professional Ashley Nicole (IG: ashnic_rawarriorfitness) is a renowned pro bodybuilding athlete, motivational speaker, author, and the founder of RA Warrior Fitness. As an autoimmune health coach, she specializes in guiding individuals through the challenges of managing conditions like rheumatoid arthritis and lupus. Ashley's journey is marked by her personal triumphs over these conditions, reflecting her commitment to enhancing her lifestyle and empowering others to do the same. Website: rawarriorfitness.com

Dr. Dawn Sheree Paramore (SM: DrDawnSheree) a licensed psychotherapist and certified trauma and prevention specialist who dedicates herself to destigmatizing mental health. Her expertise, advocacy, and motivational speaking inspire positive emotional well-being and resilience. Websites: www.DrDawnSheree.com | www.acenteredmind.com

Terolyn Phinsee is a senior software compliance manager and a community advocate for digital literacy and technology access. She is the CEO and founder of Zip & Go Assist Consulting and Titus STEAM Prep, a non-profit serving inner-city's underserved families.
Website: zipandgoassist.com

Dr. Tañia M. Reyes believes fervently in women's empowerment. She has been able to take risks all over the world without the fear of failure thanks to the unwavering support of her friends, family and sorority, Alpha Kappa Alpha. After starting Boundaries Prep Academy, No Boundaries Counseling and Consulting Firm was born. NBCCF offers a variety of services including faith-based coaching, educational advocacy, consulting and tutoring, and housing for the previously incarcerated, mentoring for teens and women, and life readiness skills. Website: www.nbccf.com

Zhelinrentice Scott, aka The SEO Queen and Lady Zhe (IG: theseoqueen), is a dynamic multi-hyphenate who is the founder and CEO of TSQ Marketing and an MIT and Goldman Sachs 10,000 Small Business Alumni. As an international jazz fusion violinist, she loves to play when she is not helping her clients own their niche online. Website: www.seoqueen.com

Shermeaka Settles is a dynamic sales manager, ordained minister, and author of *I Was Ok, As Promised*. From Macon, GA, she's a wife, mother of five, and lover of writing, reading, jazz, and history.

Natalie A. Solomon-Brimage, MPH, based in Bowie, MD (IG: meraki_empowerment_collective), is a public health practitioner and entrepreneur, specializing in women's health and cultural humility. She blends her academic background with impactful work in public health and event styling, dedicated to community wellness and inclusivity. Website: natalieasolomon-brimage.me

Verlisa Wearing, CEO of RiseHer Network (IG: verlisawearing), is a true cheerleader for all women. She encourages women to believe in themselves and their abilities. Her positive attitude and infectious energy are contagious; she inspires women to be the best versions of themselves. Website: www.verlisawearing

Albertha White Taylor is a licensed insurance agent in 43 states, First Lady, busy mom, and bestselling co-author, where she leverages her compassion and empathy to understand others and help positively inspire those in their career and personal lives.

Sharee Williams is a wife, mother, sister, aunt, cousin, friend, and motivator. She is a local herbalist, founder of 3PHASES of Becoming a Woman, and CEO of Alppha's Homecare and Holistic Services. Website: www.3phasesobaw.com

Katrenia Wright (IG and X: thewrightroad | FB: Katrenia Wright) is an award-winning rideshare driver turned bestselling author and motivational speaker who seeks simplicity: to travel, promote greatness, buy sunglasses and shoes, and eat guilt-free cake...topped with a visit to the gym. Website: www.katreniawright.com

Anthologies and Other Books
Presented by Telishia Berry

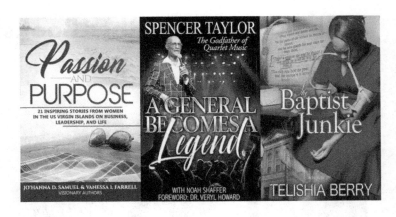

About the Publisher

Telishia Berry is the CEO of Strive Publishing and Editor-in-Chief of *Courageous Woman Magazine* and its spin-offs, *Courageous Men Magazine* and *Authors Who Launch Magazine.*

While transitioning from married to single and overcoming that stress, Telishia transformed the Courageous Woman Blog into a community print magazine with faith, determination, and the $30 she had in her bank account. The year 2023 marks twelve years of publishing more than 200 cover stories that include numerous celebrities, such as Vanessa Bell Calloway, Wendy Raquel Robinson, Mo'Nique, Sheryl Lee Ralph, Vickie Winans, Jody Watley, Claressa Shields, and Oleta Adams. As a book publisher, Telishia has helped over 400 women publish their stories and become bestselling authors.

Telishia speaks and encourages women worldwide to believe in themselves, start where they are, and use what they have to launch their products, services, and books. Telishia has deep roots in the arts. Her love for acting and performing took her around the country, performing as an actress in off-Broadway plays. She honed her skills in her first love, writing, producing, and directing theatrical productions with numerous stage plays to her credit. She is currently pitching film projects, including one based on her novel, *The Baptist Junkie*. Telishia is the recipient of multiple awards, including A Presidential Award From President Joe Biden and Kamala Harris, an Honorary Doctorate from TIUA and a Humanitarian Award, WIP Award (Women in Power), a Phenomenal Woman Award, a Resolution Award, a Publishing Excellence Award, Best Media Platform Award, Black Business Women Rock, Women in the Arts, a Write On Award, and more.

Telishia is the mother of four. Her son Kendre' Berry is a film and TV actor and music producer, most known for his role as Jabari on the TV sitcom, *Girlfriends*, and the music he performed with Quincy, produced by P. Diddy. Her three daughters are also in the entertainment industry: Tisha is a celebrity photographer (Ciara, Taraji P. Henson, Neo, Usher) and film director, Toi is a fashion model and entrepreneur, and baby girl Kennedy is a MUA and student. Telishia has one grandson, Ezra.

Subscribe to *Courageous Woman Magazine* at Courageouswomanmag.com and STRIVEIPG.com.

Follow her on IG: @courageouswomanmagazine and @Courageous_Woman_Magazine.

Made in the USA
Middletown, DE
11 April 2024

52767576R00076